Rick Wakeman

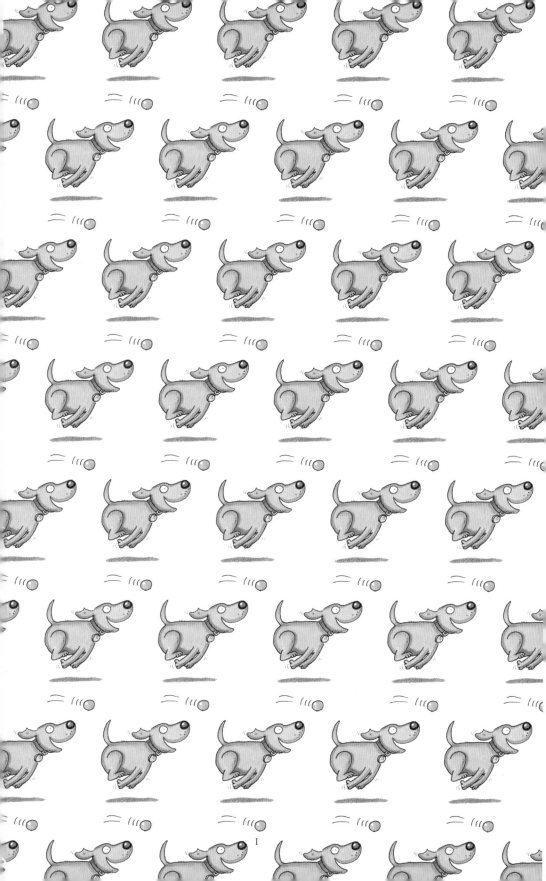

Dedicated to Yvonne, who introduced me to Alfie
one Boxing Day and changed my life again.

My Labrador Eats Poo

CHARLES

ALFIE

HARRY

Published by HaGaTaS 2017

ISBN 978-0-993-52560-5

First published in Great Britain in 2017 by HaGaTaS

A CIP catalogue record for this book is available from the British Library

Designed by Neal Townsend and Martin Cook

Illustrations © Harry Venning

My Labrador Eats Poo

A COLLECTION OF WHIMSICAL VERSES

CHARLES GARLAND

ILLUSTRATIONS BY HARRY VENNING

ACKNOWLEDGMENTS

This collection of verses would not exist but for the encouragement of
Rick Wakeman and his wife Rachel, who suggested, after poem number three,
that I write more. I have also had great positive support from
Trevor Dolby of Penguin Random House Group, dear friends Ann Croft,
Clifford King, Steve Blame, and my agent Jean Diamond.

Most of all, I have to thank my family, Father Ian, Yvonne and all our children,
Jo, Eddie, Dominic, Becky, James, Emily, and their partners and sometimes
children too. My brothers, nephews and nieces, all of whom have listened
patiently as I recited each new creation to them, and have told me by varying
degrees of reaction how much re-writing was required.

Finally, thanks are due to local friends Ro and June who promised to buy
a copy of this book, ensuring that I shift at least two.
Who can argue with figures like that?

CONTENTS

ALFIE ATE AN APPLE

Alfie ate an apple. Not a shiny Granny Smith
Or a Cox's Orange Pippin he was given for a treat.
No, this was just a windfall from our ageing garden tree
Which fell off, brown and shrivelled, and not suitable to eat.

But you cannot tell a Labrador to leave what looks so nice,
And Alfie's at his happiest with something good to chew.
He doesn't seem to mind much what it is or how it tastes,
And he loves what looks disgusting to the likes of me and you.

So this miserable apple, hard and rotten to the core,
Was the choice of snack for Alfie, and too late we saw him munch
Like a sweetie down a three-year-old it vanished in a flash
With four rancid plums completing Alfie's 'five a day' for lunch.

Two hours later Alfie threw up. Not out by the gate,
Or in a quiet corner of the garden far from view –
No. In front of all our guests, of course, in flip-flops, shorts and shirts
Enjoying Sunday sunshine while I cooked a barbeque.

The smell was quite appalling as the poor dog retched and writhed
And groaned and strained to get the wretched apple out again,
Three times we cleaned up after him, but on and on it went –
We guessed it had fermented as it caused him so much pain.

He looked so sad, his eyes were moist, he hung his head in shame
As if to say "I'm sorry" and "I won't go near that tree".
And the guests all shook their heads and said they thought it would be good
If he stuck to proper dog food and a biscuit for his tea.

Next day I took him to the vet to check that he was well.
We saw a lovely man who had a Labrador himself.
He knew what had been going on, and thought he had a bug
So he gave him an injection and a treat from his top shelf.

That afternoon our Alfie was his normal self again.
Racing round and entertaining all our guests outdoors.
Then he sneaked away – I caught him looking furtive by the gate
With a huge, brown, rotting apple firmly gripped between his jaws.

THE KITCHEN CLOCK

Alfie's in the kitchen
And he's gazing at the wall –
So why choose cold hard lino
Not the carpet in the hall?
He looks up at the kitchen clock
The seconds ticking past,
I expect that he is hoping
That it's dinner time at last.

MY LABRADOR EATS POO

The sun is shining gloriously, with white clouds drifting by.
The fields all sway with ripening corn, beneath an azure sky,
And Alfie's eager for a walk, I really love it too
But one thing always spoils it, my labrador eats poo.

His habit starts with rabbit, it's like caviar for dogs
In little dark brown tasty spheres, instead of chocolate logs.
And if a horse has passed this way, he'll feast upon that too.
There's no way I can stop him – my labrador eats poo.

I've tried to keep him on the lead, distract him with a treat,
But every time he sniffs it out, his favourite thing to eat.
Last week he ate a pigeon; head, bones and feathers too
But that was only second best, my labrador eats poo.

I have to clean the garden up every day or two,
Collect the 'waste' in plastic bags, a smelly job to do.
And by my side he ambles, as he's nothing else to do,
Ignoring all the ones *he* did, my labrador eats poo.

However much I beg and plead and tell him what to do,
However much I tell him "leave!" and "shush" and "whoosh" and "shoo!"
The future's looking hopeless, may I ask advice of you?
Do you know how to stop the way my labrador eats poo?

So if you come to visit, you will see this handsome hound
With gleaming coat and wagging tail and happy panting sound.
Although he's cute, don't let him lick or kiss you like they do
For he hides a dreadful secret … my labrador eats poo.

OUR FIRST WALK

I was feeling so excited when I woke up on the day
That our labrapup was old enough to leave the house and play.
He'd been to see our lovely vet to get those puppy jabs
That look like noxious liquids, brewed by scientists in labs.

Now when I mentioned "labs" then, it's not short for 'Labrador'
It's 'laboratory', but let's not pause, semantics are a bore.
And when I mentioned 'pause' then, that's not the 'paws' like feet –
Oh blast, we're back to word play. Give in. Admit defeat.
'Defeat' are not … OK, I'll stop and get on with my tale.
Which isn't like the wagging one … oh lock me up in jail!

So anyway. The little chap was spinning round and round.
Chewing on his brand new lead, and churning up the ground.
He was ready for a walk, the first we'd ever shared
Beyond the safe old garden fence through which he'd only stared.

So off we went, the dog and me – he couldn't get it right!
Our walk was so erratic it looked more like a fight.
I thought we'd go along the path towards a wood I'd found,
But Alfie didn't do straight lines, his choice was round and round.
I didn't care, we both had fun, and Alfie looked so grand,
So I offered him a biscuit, and he grinned, and bit my hand.

MY LABRADOR'S DYSPRAXIC

My Labrador's dyspraxic – he rushes here and there
Crashing into furniture as if it wasn't there.
And when he's quite exhausted from bounding to and fro
He settles down to gnawing all the tassels off the throw.
What's more he doesn't notice when a table goes for six
To him it's just a chewing board held up with tasty sticks.

My Labrador's dyspraxic – especially round the tail
If there's a cup in striking range he'll hit it without fail.
He plunges into puddles and is desperate to share
The cool refreshing water, so he shakes it everywhere.
And if you're really lucky, he will rub himself quite dry
On the article of clothing which cost the most to buy.

My Labrador's dyspraxic – he chucks himself about
Like a grinning whirling dervish crossed with a lager lout.
He doesn't mean to break things, don't think he doesn't care
He's just a normal Labrador, not spatially aware.
But you can't be cross with Alfie, he just doesn't realise
That he's not a little puppy, he's a whirlwind in disguise.

A DAY IN LONDON

I have to go to London, to meet a man I know.
It's not just round the corner, it's quite a way to go.
But my friend is always charming, and we'll have a bite to eat,
We'll talk and laugh and drink some wine – a day you couldn't beat.

The only tricky moment comes as I head for the door,
And hear a little whimper from my friend down on the floor.
He looks at me with big sad eyes, I know I must be strong,
"Be good" I say "I promise that I won't be very long"

His tail begins to thump as if to say "You go and play –
But I'll be waiting for you here, so don't be gone all day."

A PERFECT DAY ...

Imagine this. A perfect day, the sun is blazing down
And everyone is grateful that we don't live in the town.
The birds are singing, bees are buzzing, everything is calm
It seems that nothing could occur to cause us any harm.

Then.

The sound of splashing gives us all a twenty second warning
If we don't rush to get inside he'll ruin our peaceful morning.
From Lavenham to Lakenheath, from Elvedon to Eye,
It will set the people talking as we raise a hue and cry,
From Bildeston to Braintree, to Norwich and beyond
They will hear the dreadful warning – "Alfie's in the pond!"

We make the safety of the door in sixteen seconds flat,
Congratulate ourselves on having senses like a cat.
"You moved so fast!" "You got there first!" "So agile and so supple!"
"You wouldn't think to see you move you've had more than a couple!"
And panting at the window with a hint of trepidation
Our nostrils are assaulted by stinking, rotting vegetation.

A two-tone dog emerges, blond on top and black beneath
The odour of the stagnant water's grim beyond belief.
Little clumps of dying pond weed hang down from his belly
A lily pad adorns his collar – he's soaking wet and smelly.

And then the awful truth dawns like a film slow motion scene
There are gasps of shock and horror and some "oh no's" in between.
Alfie is advancing on the washing line, that's full
Of blouses, skirts and crisp white shirts, clean cotton, linen, wool.

He's just about to shake and ruin hours of careful work
When he stops. And turns. And I detect a canny canine smirk.
He's seen another target – in our haste we left him there …
It's Grandpa! Gently snoring, and completely unaware.

We shout, and try to stop the monster sizing up his prey
But far too late, he's met his fate in a stinking, soaking spray.
A bucketful of droplets fall as Alfie shakes again.
The dear man wakes, and smiles, and says "Was that a spot of rain?"

ALFIE AND THE BALLOON

It was a freezing cold New Year's Day,
the ground was solid and white.
We went for a walk in our usual way,
and saw a curious sight.
For rounding a windswept corner
was a remnant from somebody's 'do' –
A large red balloon tied with seasonal string
but no label to say who it's to.

In the centre of the frozen field
you might have expected a rabbit.
A sugar beet maybe, but not a balloon,
so Alfie rushed over to grab it
He went twenty yards and then stopped.
As if he was trying to decide
On a plan of attack from the front or the back
or if it was better to hide

He looked back for re-assurance,
so I shouted "Go on! Fetch it here!"
He went ten more yards, and then as before
he seemed overcome by his fear.
I called him again to encourage,
and give him the will to go on,
So he started to stalk with a mysterious walk
as though all his worry had gone.

The balloon bounced around agitated,
as though it were trying to get free
But Alf took the plunge with a brilliant lunge,
dispatched it to eternity.
It went off with a bang like a gunshot!
Which made Alfie leap in the air –
He rushed to my side open-mouthed and wild-eyed
at the speed of a terrified hare.

I laughed like a drain when I saw him,
for when the balloon had gone down
It had superimposed on the end of his nose,
so he looked like a Labrador clown
I wished I had christened him 'Rudolf' –
he resembled the reindeer-in-chief
I'll remember that look and I'll auction this book
and donate it to Comic Relief.

ALFIE AND THE DAFFODIL

Alfie has three hobbies – walk, and sniff, and eat.
But never in that order, try offering him a treat!
I would have added sleeping, but that's a way of life
He slides gently into slumber like butter off a knife.
His head goes down, his tail lies still, and with contented sighs
He slips into a doggy trance with still half open eyes.
Food is an obsession, and when he goes to sleep
I'm sure he pictures tasty treats instead of counting sheep.

Sniffing on the other hand requires full concentration.
His mind's alert, his nostrils twitch in acute anticipation.
He's really just a nose on legs, his senses are so keen
He'll stick his snout in everything unless I intervene
He loves the smells of people best, old shoes, old socks, old feet
And parts you wish he wouldn't sniff the moment you first meet.

One April morning we were out and heading for the wood
When Alfie smelled a brand new smell he thought was really good.
He tugged his lead and strained to find the source of this new pong
He studied every blade of grass, but always got it wrong.

The scent came from a daffodil – alas the stupid hound
Was searching at the roots and had his nose pressed to the ground.
He started getting cross, he growled and scratched at the plant's base
Until his human mummy pushed the flower in his face.
His reaction was hilarious. His chin sank to his chest,
His tail went between his legs, he didn't seem impressed.

Of course we reassured him, said he didn't need to fear it,
We stroked his head, said "good boy", but he still would not go near it.
And so we picked the daffodil to prove it caused no harm
And Alfie slowly raised his head while we stood quiet and calm.
He plucked up courage, gave a sniff, but the pollen made him cough
So he ate it. Swallowed it in one, and happy, trotted off.

ALFIE AND THE WOLF

Alfie saw a wolf today, just by our own back door
At first he froze, his hackles rose, and then he hit the floor.
He lay quite flat and hid behind a handy human being
So I'd be bitten first, by the wolf we both were seeing.
Alfie's quite a brave dog under normal circumstances
But faced with such a fierce beast he wasn't taking chances.

To be quite honest, I was scared. The wolf just licked its lips
I felt a tiny dampness growing in between my hips.
And then a lovely lady came, and giving me a grin
Walked calmly over to the wolf and tickled its huge chin.
The wolf stopped snarling instantly and looked up at our saviour
Who said she hoped he hadn't been displaying bad behaviour.

"He's a JAPANESE AKITA" she said, "A friendly chap"
I didn't say her wolf had caused an embarrassing mishap.
Alfie looked much better now he even wagged his tail
And sniffed the wolf's most private bits – a plan that couldn't fail.
Within ten seconds off they ran and played so happily
I smiled nicely at the lady and invited her to tea.

I know you think I'm daft – it was a genuine mistake
And Alfie thought the same, it was a wolf, for heaven's sake.
The lady gave a fancy name to hide the truth from us
She probably was much amused observing all the fuss.
We're meeting in the park next week, and just to irritate her
I'll take my "EVERGLADE ABITER" – he's a four foot alligator.

WET WALKS

It's a windy Wednesday morning and the rain is chucking down –
We like that in the country, unlike people in the town.
It makes the crops grow faster, swells potatoes, peas and beet.
We never mind the feel of soggy grass beneath our feet.

We haven't any pavements so we walk along the track
And have to wipe the mud off dirty paws when we get back.
Alfie's tail is always wagging even though the sky's not blue,
He looks at me, I know he's thinking 'I don't care, do you?'

ALFIE'S GIRL-FRIEND

Alfie's got a girl-friend
I have to call her this –
A bitch-friend just sounds terrible
And looks like prejudice.

They both subscribe to Facebook
And their profiles look all right
But I've not heard Alfie typing
Or Skyping in the night.

I don't know how they do it,
Swapping woofs and chat up whines
But there's something sexy going on
If you read between the lines.

Poor Alfie is a virgin
And he's lost his vital parts
But that doesn't stop him dreaming
Of romance and flowers and hearts.

He gazes at her photograph
I know he's got the hots
Let's hope his teenage lusting
Doesn't bring him out in spots

Her name is Grace – she's really cute
And though I don't intrude
I'm sure I hear him saying "Grace"
Before he eats his food.

CHRISTMAS CHEER

We had barely had our breakfast
When the doorbell rang, again.
First the paper, then the milkman,
Next the postman. What a pain.
Six more times the wretched doorbell
Rang, so I ran to the door.
Was the house on fire? I wondered
What would police arrest me for?

On the step a po-faced courier
Rang the doorbell one more time
As I stood there! Quite defiant,
Maybe earning overtime.
"Can I help you?" I asked sweetly
putting on a loveless smile
"Garland?" "Yes" He threw a parcel
at my feet. The smell was vile.

Someone sent us cheese for Christmas
From a shop in Saint Omer
Advertising it would only
Take one day to get it there.
On the box, in French and English
Plus rapide the cheese express.
Guaranteed! it boasted boldly
How, is anybody's guess.

What they couldn't know, and sadly
Didn't then anticipate
Was snow and frost and ice and hailstones
Making their delivery late.
Three long days it sat in Calais
With the train stuck to the line
Six more mislaid at St Pancras
Caused the odours to combine.

As you know, the sense of smell
Is ten times better in a dog.
They can smell a tiny insect
Hiding deep inside a log.
They can sense a trace of turkey
Lurking on a Christmas fork,
Or a scrap of un-smoked bacon
Wrapped around a scratch of pork.

Labradors have one obsession
Every owner knows this well –
Food. In every shape and form
From burgers through to béchamel.
They're not fussy, Cornflakes, catfish,
Carrots, crusts and Cottage pies,
Quiche and chicken, even dog food
Disappear before your eyes.

Imagine, if you can, young Alfie
With the courier at the door,
How his little nose reacted
To the package on the floor.
He went wild. He whined and pined
His tail went round and round with glee.
Longingly he looked up to me
Saying "is that box for me?"

He followed me into the kitchen
Watched as all the children fled
Holding noses, all complaining
That it smelled like something dead.
He alone anticipated
Glorious morsels shared with me –
Camembert that oozes outwards
Runny Pont L'Eveque and Brie.

Cheese that follows when you whistle
Cheese to make a Frenchman proud!
Sacre bleu! C'est magnifique!
Sing the Marseillaise out loud!
Nothing pasteurised or processed,
Coated with a plastic rind,
Nothing bland or namby-pamby,
Just the finest you can find.

Smiling broadly I arranged them
On my largest chopping board.
Carefully as I unwrapped them
I admired my cheesy hoard.
Happily I found the biscuits,
Joyously I broke the bread,
French baguette I'd made for breakfast
Gallic odours filled my head.

Faithful Alfie sat there waiting
Patiently on my left shoe.
Concentrating, watching, hoping
He could share this bounty too.
Loyal ally, to rely on,
He and I appreciate
Haute cuisine in all its glory
Spreading out across my plate.

Butter is not needed here,
Tautologically too much.
Just a glass of Chateau Margaux
Adds the final perfect touch.
Alf and I had lunch together.
A morsel here, a biscuit there.
All the rest went out for pizza.
Yes, you guessed it, we don't care!

A NORMAL DAY

It seems just like a normal day. A Tuesday, warm and dry.
"I've had enough of work" I say, "Let's kiss the desk goodbye.
No guilt, no tearful fare-thee-wells, just go with no delay,
Slip on the lead and off we go – it's time to seize the day".
Across the road, across the field, to paths the rabbits mow,
Between the gorse and bracken, where the roe and fallow go.
A paradise of different smells from creatures great and small,
And Alfie's pulling at his lead, he wants to sniff them all.
I let him go, and off he runs – it always makes me smile,
I'm glad to see that Alfie's keen to go the extra mile.
At last he trots back to my side with panting, happy grin.
I know he's had a lovely run, it's time to go back in.
Then for the first time he cocks his leg!
His crouching days are through!
At last he's like a grown up boy,
And as I praise him, full of joy,
He piddles on my shoe.

BIG YELLOW DOG

Big yellow dog
Sleeping like a log
Dreaming of the moment
When he's going to get some food
Visitors arrive
Alfie comes alive
Sniffs the lady's bottom
Which is really very rude.

People sitting down
Alfie starts to frown
Why is no-one stroking me
The way I like them to?
Better muscle in
Wag my tail and grin –
Lady gets a blast of breath
Like only doggies do.

Guests go away
Didn't have to say
Lady feeling queasy,
'cos we already knew …
Won't see them again
Two less to entertain
That's what comes of having
A dog who eats poo.

I HAVE A LITTLE NUT TREE

I have a little nut tree,
Nothing does it bear
Except some little plastic bags
That I've left hanging there.

When I take Alfie for a walk,
He has to have a poo
And I put it in a little bag
The way good owners do.

I can't pretend it doesn't smell
And it sticks like lumps of glue
So I wouldn't want to take it
On a two mile walk, would you?

I have to put it somewhere
Where it won't get left behind
When I'm walking, bags of dog poo
Aren't the first thing on my mind.

And so I hang the little bags
On the branches of a tree
Which on our way back down the lane
I cannot fail to see.

It sounds so simple, doesn't it?
Before we go back in
Take all the bags down from the tree
And put them in the bin.

But sometimes my mind wanders
And we go walking past
Forgetting all about the bags –
By now they're growing fast.

Four days go by. The little tree
Looks like it needs a prune.
A couple more, you'd think that Christmas
Had come six months too soon.

I don't know what the neighbours think
Or if they laugh or curse
The sight is odd, but oh my god
The smell is ten times worse.

Eventually I wake up
And remember what I've done
I sneak out with a bin bag
Before the day's begun.

Then Alfie gets an early walk
And he seems quite impressed
He wrinkles up his nose, and loves
The smell we all detest.

The King of Spain's daughter
Wouldn't want to visit me –
In case I have forgotten
To unload the nut tree.

IDENTITY CRISIS

Alfie must have looked in a mirror
Or seen his reflection in a glass door –
Because, for the last few days I think
He's wondering why he's a Labrador.
Perhaps it's just an identity crisis
Experienced by teenage girls and boys,
Torn between being cool and clubbing
And staying at home with sweets and toys.

Well, Alfie appears dissatisfied
With being the golden dog he is,
And considering which other breed he could be
Is putting the poor thing into a tizz
I think he's trying a couple of options
(He may just react to the phase of the moon)
I'll try to describe the way he's been acting
And hope he goes back to his normal self soon.

Alfie thinks he's a greyhound.
Out on our walk today
We saw a hare sitting quietly
Ahead on the path, in our way.
Alfie started running
As fast as his legs would go,
But the hare just sat there watching
As if it was saying "and so?"

When Alfie was almost upon it
The hare took off in a flash.
It completed a hundred metres
Like a record Olympian dash.
Poor Alfie sat down quite exhausted
Watching the hare recede,
It must have seemed quite amazing to him
An animal reaching such speed.

The hare looked round with a challenge
"Come on then, fat dog, let's race!"
But Alfie's above such an insult.
With a dignified look on his face,
And an air of superiority
He turned, with his head held high,
And ambled back to the pathway
To the biscuit which told him "nice try"

*   *   *

Alfie thinks he's a bloodhound.
Out on our walk today
He was wandering round with his nose to the ground
In a most unusual way.
I like to go out for an hour
And cover a mile or two
But he lagged behind, canine mastermind,
As though he was hunting a clue.

He examined all of the evidence
Of who had passed by that day.
He sniffed every clod, every sod where we trod
Compiling his dossier.
At last he seemed to have cracked it
He lifted his head with a glance
Which said, I supposed,
"I declare the case closed
It was nothing but circumstance".

*   *   *

Alfie thinks he's a spaniel.
The sort with the long floppy ears
That leap into water when they didn't ought-a
And the smell never quite disappears.
We went for our walk in the morning,
There'd been lots of rain in the night –
Pretty soon I discovered the puddles had covered
The whole of the path on the right.

So I headed off for the left side,
But Alfie thought it would be fun
To try to be boss and drag me across
And soak me in every one.
He was so quick he caught me off balance
And I had the lead round my wrist
So he pulled and I jerked, but his strategy worked,
So I tried to jump – but I missed.

ALFIE AND THE BIG POND

We went to the beach for the afternoon
The first time that Alfie had been
His first impression was, I think,
'That's the biggest pond I've ever seen'

He couldn't wait to get down the path
His tail was wagging like mad
And we were all happy, in a summer so wet
On the best sunny day that we'd had.

Now when we're out walking and meet other dogs
Alfie runs up to sniff and say 'Hi!'
But on this afternoon he ignored the whole lot
And looking straight forward, rushed by.

At last we arrived at the foot of the cliff
And walked to the dog friendly bit
Then on to the sand, Alfie's paws sinking in
Oh, the joy of just rolling in it.

To double our fun we'd arranged for our Alf
To play with a friend on the shore.
Our nephew and niece with their parents arrived
With Bonnie, they'd not met before.

Bonnie's a young springer spaniel
With a permanent grin on her face
Who ought to enrol in athletics events –
She would probably win every race.

Now Alfie prefers a relaxed way of life,
Taking life at a leisurely rate
But seeing young Bonnie race hither and yon
Inspired him to participate.

He chased after Bonnie and ran up and down
And found it all glorious fun
Then Bonnie decided she felt a bit hot
After rushing around in the sun.

She lives near the coast, and is used to the sea,
So ran in, tail wagging, to play –
Alfie followed, not knowing what happens out there
With the salt and the waves and the spray.

At first glance it looked like the pond at his home
Apart from the difference in size
It all looked quite calm for a minute or two
But behind him there lurked a surprise

He turned round to see us, just like a small kid
"Look at me mum, I'm here in the sea!"
Then the biggest of waves broke right over his head
Poor Alfie was wet as can be.

The water ran back and he sat on the sand
With some seaweed still stuck to his face.
"A pond that fights back! What nightmare is this?
You know, I've gone right off this place."

ALFIE SITS

Alfie sits with his back to me. I really don't know why,
But he seems to find it difficult to look me in the eye.
He's totally contented when I scratch behind his ear,
But I have to lean right over as his head is not that near.

He's happy when he's stretching out and resting on my knee,
But he always looks the other way and never up at me.
I've asked around, but no-one else has problems like I do,
Their Labradors all sit and face them. Alfie, why don't you?

I'd like to see his profile; he's a canine thoroughbred,
But all I'm ever offered is the back of Alfie's head.
I think he has such classic looks, which show his pedigree –
But perhaps this noble creature doesn't think the same of me …

WHEN ALFIE MET A ROCK STAR

As far as Alfie was concerned it was just another day
We'd been out for our morning walk the same as yesterday.
And then the doorbell rang, and Alfie rushed into the hall
"A visitor! Hooray! A chance to play! Now where's my ball?"
I called him back and shut him in, not everyone is fond
Of being jumped on by a hairy canine vagabond.
The visitor came in, and we all had a cup of tea.

And then he said, "There's someone missing – come on, where is he?
Where's Alfie?" and I knew then it wasn't really me
That this famous rock musician had travelled here to see.
We went into the kitchen, I thought Alfie would jump up
And beg for fussing, just the way he used to as a pup.

But Alf was not expecting a human quite this tall!
This guy is really massive, while I am rather small.
Alfie just looked up at him, and up, and up, until
He saw the rock star's golden locks – "A cousin! What a thrill!"
Although it was embarrassing, I have to tell the truth –
That Alfie's form of greeting strangers can be quite uncouth.

Like all boy dogs he likes to sniff a human's 'private bits',
And Alfie did just that this day, while I had forty fits.
The rock star took it in his stride, and making friends, he said
"I know a lot about you Alf" and stroked his big blonde head.
Just then a tiny spider came from underneath a chair
And headed for the window as if no-one else was there.

Immediately distracted, Alfie's nose went to the floor,
He had to check it out, because he'd not seen one before.
He totally ignored our guest, which I thought rather rude –
The sort of thing he does when it's approaching time for food.
So I apologised for Alfie. It was clear to see
That for him a spider's twice as nice as a celebrity.

OUT TO LUNCH

I've so looked forward to today, because I have a hunch
That the boss is on his way right now to take me out to lunch.
He always dresses nicely in his wellies and his hat
And he puts my harness on and tells me that I'm getting fat.

Then off we go together walking slowly to the wood –
For restaurants at lunchtime it's the finest neighbourhood.
It's time to choose a starter. Should I leave some room for pud?
Whichever one I pick I know it's going to be good.

It has to be the rabbit – the choice is very clear
According to my nose there's half a rabbit lying near.
The boss unclips my harness and it's time to start to eat –
And I was right, the starter's there, just ten steps from my feet.

I grab it in an instant but I'll eat it on my own.
The boss will skip the first course, busy on his mobile phone.
Some lovely bunny crunching and the rabbit's down the hatch.
I'm ready for the main course, and it's in that nettle patch.

They have a choice of specials here to tempt a dog today,
There's squirrel, rat or pheasant leg to munch along the way.
I think I'll have the partridge. It suits my palate best,
And I love the way the juices dribble down on to my chest.

Uh-oh – the boss has seen me. So now begins the fun.
He doesn't fancy partridge, so I think I'd better run.
I'll get a hundred yards ahead so when he reaches me
I'll have finished what I'm eating and be ready for course three.

He doesn't look too happy when he gets to where I sit,
So I'll have to wag my tail and pant and grovel just a bit.
If I can look appealing and gaze lovingly at him
He'll probably forgive me, and he'll laugh and say I'm dim.

He thinks I'm just a stomach on four paws without a brain
He doesn't give me credit for self catering again.
I supplement my diet from the fields round our house
There's protein in abundance from a deer to a mouse.

I'm saving him a fortune but he doesn't seem to care.
Hold on – I think my third course is lurking over there.
I bound across the ditch to see what morsels I can find
It's a hedgehog, and I don't think lunch is foremost in his mind.

He rolls up like a spiky ball. He looks just like a toy!
Perhaps he wants to play with me? I assume that he's a boy.
I cannot see a girlhog behaving in this way,
She'd want to comb her spikes and plan her summer holiday.

I'll start by giving him a sniff, but OUCH! I've hit a spike!
It's sticking in my nose and it's a feeling I don't like.
It really hurts – thank heavens that the boss is standing near.
I'll run across and hope he'll see the problem I have here.

I sit down and I whimper, and now he's bending down,
Examining my nose and wearing such a puzzled frown.
At last he's sees the spine and in a jiffy pulls it out.
Oh sweet relief, the pain has gone and I can lick my snout.

It's put me right off eating lunch, I'd rather just go back.
My appetite has gone now, and it's time to hit the sack.
We wander home, and soon I'm dreaming of the lovely fun
I had when master took me out to have lunch on the run.

ALFIE THE PHILOSOPHER

Alfie's lying on the sofa
Fast asleep at half past six.
In his dreams he's chasing rabbits
Running fast and catching sticks.
Sometimes he gives out a whimper
Asking for another treat.
Eyelids flicker, twitching quicker
With his sleeping running feet.
Soon his r.e.m. is finished
Serious snoring then ensues,
Rattling like a jowly jumbo
High on fags and too much booze.

How can Alfie be so tired?
All he's done is sleep and eat.
Twice a day a country ramble
Makes his schedule quite complete.
Why is Alfie so exhausted?
Comatose since ten to five.
Where's his dogged animation?
Vigour, energy and drive?
Perhaps he's thinking deeply,
Pondering philosophy,
Canine existential questions …
Or he's waiting for his tea.

ALFIE'S PENGUIN

Alfie had a penguin held lightly in his jaws.
He gave a look as if to say "this penguin's mine, not yours"
He ran off to the kitchen, and threw it on his bed,
Then pounced on it and shook it, brought his paw down on its head.
And then he licked its little face and lay down with a sigh.
A happy boy, contented dog, and easy to see why.

The penguin in the meantime didn't even squeak –
It was not the sort of penguin that someone made to speak.
It lay there next to Alfie with a smiling, scarlet beak,
A bright green woolly hat and scarf, and tubby, squat physique.
Alfie loves his penguin – the penguin's happy too,
For now that Christmastime has passed, he's something new to do.

It's so much better than last year. When January came
He went into a wooden box, which seemed a rotten shame.
He stayed there with the Santa Claus, where nobody could see
The Christmas lights, the stockings, or the baubles for the tree.
He lay there for eleven months until the happy day
When it was winter, time again for toys to come and play.

But this year it's all different! He's happy as a lark.
He's cuddled up to Alfie, and not lying in the dark.
I said "don't eat the penguin!" Alfie seemed to understand,
He brought his new toy over and he put him in my hand.
Good dog. You play with penguin, lovely gentle Labrador,
And he will be your best friend 'till it's Christmastime one more.

SLUMBERING LABRADOR

Alfie is an office dog, he has his own black chair
So all I have to do is turn my head to see him there.
He snores a lot, but I don't mind, it means he is content,
Not asking for a walk or food, he's in his element.
But even in his deepest sleep if I should say his name
He's up, awake, and by my side and ready for a game.
A ball, a stick, he doesn't mind, providing at the end
There's a carrot or a rice cake, as a prize from his best friend.

Alfie Wellington is the grandson of "Carpenny Walpole" who was Great British Champion, International Champion, and Nordic Champion. If you should meet Alfie, please don't mention this, as he's quite modest about it. His great-great-grandfather was called "CornlandsWellington", and he's happy to carry on this family tradition.

Born and bred in Suffolk, he enjoys walks with Charles, who spent most of his childhood wandering about in the Suffolk countryside.

The Real Alfie

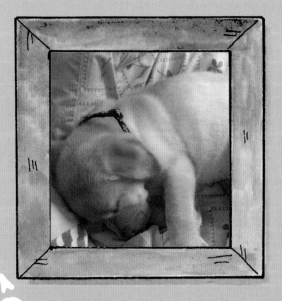

Charles Garland has had a diverse career including working as an actor; writer; producer, director, composer; cabaret artist; singer/guitarist; organist; campanologist; after dinner speaker and beetroot boiler. Despite starting professional life as a very short dancer in a musical, situation comedy has been his main interest. He has written a large number of comedies, none of which has ever been shown, but all of which have titles ending with an exclamation mark. This neat trick was learned from David Croft OBE.

My Labrador Eats Poo

THE AUDIO VERSION OF EVERYTHING FROM THE FIRST BOOK

- PLUS AN EXTRA BONUS OF VERSES FROM BOOK TWO

PIANO INTERLUDES BY RICK WAKEMAN

Enjoy more of Alfie's world as he becomes a sulky
teenager and puts on too much weight...

Available soon from Amazon, all good bookshops and record shops

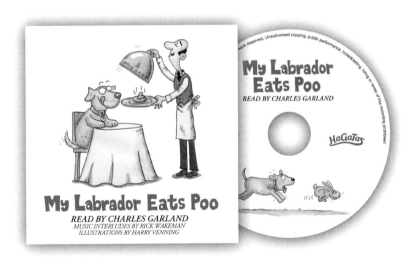